The Roots of Pentecostalism and the Charismatic Movement

Moreno Dal Bello

THE ROOTS OF PENTECOSTALISM AND THE CHARISMATIC MOVEMENT

The Pentecostal/Charismatic movement owes a very great deal to the early Black Holiness Churches. Black Holiness Pentecostalism, which formed between 1885 and 1916 "... *is not a denomination but rather a movement encompassing several denominations professing belief in Spirit baptism accompanied by several signs including speaking in tongues, with historic roots embracing, but not always restricted to, both a Wesleyan-Arminian and finished work of Calvary orientation. Participants believe that the baptism in the Holy Spirit is a normative post-conversion experience available to all Christians for the purpose of becoming more effective witnesses in carrying out the Great Commission"* ('Dictionary of Pentecostal and Charismatic Movements', p. 77). This is rather ironical to say the least, since the true Gospel of God was never preached by this movement. These Black Holiness Churches were the breeding ground from which sprang the modern-day Pentecostal/Charismatic movement: *"Perhaps more than any other twentieth-century religious movement in the West, Black Holiness-Pentecostalism is regarded by many as a highly significant catalyst and spawning ground for scores of denominations including the Charismatic renewal, all emphasizing the centrality of the Holy*

Spirit. _So little attention had been given to Black Holiness-Pentecostalism by historians that Lutheran theologian Dietrich Bonhoeffer, while visiting the U.S. from Germany, referred to its participants as the 'step-children of modern church history'"_('Dictionary of Pentecostal and Charismatic Movements', p.77).

Very few publications, be they Christian or secular and for reasons known only to them, have ever touched on the curious connection between those early Black Holiness Churches, from which Pentecostalism and Charismaticism emerged, and the Voodoo religion of those very black men and women that made up these early gatherings. The word _Voodoo_ is derived from a West African word for _God_. The above mentioned Dictionary of Pentecostal and Charismatic movements, a pro-Charismatic and Pentecostal publication, admits: " _...it appears from the evidence that Black Holiness-Pentecostalism shares the legacy of black slave religion, whose historic roots are anchored deep in African and Afro-Caribbean religion_" (p.77), the most prominent African and Afro-Caribbean religion being Voodoo. **And this is the movement that fathered the Charismatic and Pentecostal movements of today!** Not only was the Black Holiness movement filled with false signs and lying wonders, it also promoted the satanically inspired gospel of John Wesley's Arminian way, and had within its constitution all sorts of traditions and practices carried over from the Voodoo religion.

Several years ago a little-known, yet highly significant, article entitled, *'Hear That Long Snake Moan'*, appeared in the progressive *L.A. Weekly*. Written by Michael Ventura in the Spring of 1987, it shed much light on the origins and ancestry of the modern-day Pentecostal /Charismatic movements. Here are some extremely revealing excerpts from this article: *"W.E.B. DuBois described black Christianist religion as a meeting of three elements: 'The Preacher, the Music, and the Frenzy.' <u>It is in the frenzy that, with both black and white fundamentalists, we find African Voodoo absolutely intact, with merely the symbols changed.</u> The object of the Voodoo ceremony is possession by the god. Possession by the Holy Ghost is as much 'a formal goal of the religion' in Holiness and Pentecostal churches as possession is in Voodoo. Writes Paul Oliver in his 'Songsters and Saints': 'Placing himself in the hands of God, the supplicant sought possession by the Holy Spirit...Glossolalia, or uttering unintelligible syllables believed to be the language of the Holy Ghost, was evidence to many that the speaker was possessed by the Holy Spirit...and this was an essential part of the process of sanctification. People possessed of the Spirit in church might 'fall out' in a trance and might even require to be forcibly held down or controlled until they came around.'"*

Ventura adds that one man named Metraux, *"...observed the relationship, too, saying that 'a pentecostal preacher describing his feelings when 'the spirit was upon him,' listed to me exactly the same symptoms as those which I heard from the mouths of people who had been possessed by the 'loa' (gods)...Undeniably the ecstasy which breaks out during the ceremonies of certain Protestant sects in the South of the United States reflects a survival, if not of the rites, then at least of religious behaviour"* (p.43). Voodoo customs and traditions were kept very much alive by the black slaves who had been shipped to America in the nineteenth century. They would often drum the voodoo rhythms in the cotton fields and sing. When the slave masters discovered what they were doing, they outlawed the drumming. In place of this, the Voodoo-devoted black slaves turned to tapping out the voodoo beat using their feet through what we know today as tap-dancing. This satanic, beat driven music is continued today in Charismatic assemblies through its use of Rock 'n' Roll, a style of music which has indisputable links with Voodoo, as is attested by some of the world's leading secular musicians. It was from this very Voodoo slave religion that a *"...'black style' of worship developed in an unstructured way....it was the slave's adaption to Christianity without being completely divested of his native religious worship style that later proved to be significant in its impact on black religious lifestyle"* ('Dictionary of Pentecostal and Charismatic Movements', p.77).

Michael Ventura makes a further comment on the disturbing similarities between the manifestations and occurrences during Voodoo ceremonies and early Black Holiness-Pentecostal gatherings: *"The wild movements of the 'horse' mounted by the godly 'rider'; the wild speech, including speaking in tongues which in Haiti is sometimes referred to as 'talking with Africa'; the unpredictability of the possession, how, excited by the music, the frenzy can strike people who don't want it and don't believe in it* (this is a common occurrence in Charismatic meetings, especially the Toronto Blessing meetings where many who doubted and disbelieved the veracity of the phenomena occurring in those meetings suddenly found themselves rolling about on the floor in hysterical and uncontrolled laughter), *you find all of these central Voodoo phenomena in most black and white fundamentalist churches* (needless to say the author here is referring to those Pentecostal and Charismatic Fundamentalist churches). *Maya Deren tells of first resisting and then being overpowered by a god during a ceremony she was observing..."* (p. 43). Interesting to note that it has been reported by some people who have been present with those who were experimenting with drugs such as LSD, but who had not themselves partaken of it, that suddenly and without warning they, too, began to experience the effects of the drug which others had taken but which they had refused, showing that a spiritual experience was taking place. This same phenomena is reported by many who have attended charismatic meetings as mere observers. Suddenly, they too experienced being 'slain in the spirit' or speaking in 'tongues', unable to control their mouths (one woman needed to have a towel stuffed in her mouth in order to stop her 'tongues' speaking!), or rolling about on the floor in hysterical laughter, some people even trying to divest themselves of their clothing. A spiritual experience *is* taking place, but the spirit behind it all is NOT the Holy Spirit of God.

In more recent times, there appeared on the scene a woman named Agnes Ozman who, on January 1, 1901, whilst enrolled at the Bethel Bible College of Pentecostalism co-founder Charles F. Parham, in Topeka, Kansas, claimed to have received the gift of tongues just as it was given on the day of Pentecost. What ensued was what would later become known as the Azusa St. meetings, which began in 1907 and were attended by people from all over the world, much like the infamous 'Toronto Blessing' meetings in our own day to which people foolishly flock. Even now many, if not most, Charismatics believe that the series of meetings at Azusa St., which were held three times a day, seven days a week and went on for years, was a *second* Pentecost, but as the following quotes **from the very founders of Pentecostalism** no less and other eye-witnesses will show, these venerated meetings were far from godly and in accordance with biblical order or precedent. The following is an eye-witness account of what occurred at Azusa St. one evening: *"When I visited the Azusa St. Mission, the first person to attract my attention was a woman with a thin, white silk waist on, who stood shaking from head to foot...There were several* *rows of chairs in front of her that were filled with seekers. The coloured leader, Seymour, was preaching; but I could not keep my eyes off the woman who continued to shake until a man in front of her slid down out of his chair and became unconscious. I then lost sight of the woman. The man who fell in a vision was pale and thin, and under high nerve pressure, and continued in the same position on the floor until after a number of seekers had gathered around the altar. Then he arose, staggered to them and began to shake his hand in front of their faces and wave his arms over their heads and moan. He was still apparently in a half-conscious state. Then he put his hands on the heads of the women and began to shake their hair. Some of them lost control of themselves and went under a hypnotic spell. He rubbed a man's jaw until the victim tumbled over on the floor and lay for half an hour, then suddenly began to jabber. Those who had received their 'Pentecost' cried out, 'He has the baptism, he has the baptism!'"* I challenge anyone to find for me a biblical precedent for any of this that was Holy Spirit-inspired and not a display of demonic-inspired lunacy! Only the naive, the gullible and the ignorant could possibly be deceived by such madness into thinking that they were in the presence, and under the influence, of the Holy Spirit.

The eye-witness account continues: *"A young colored woman, doing her best to get the gibberish, went through all kinds of contortions in her efforts to get her tongue to work. While work among the seekers at the altar was going on, a colored woman had her arms around a white man's neck, praying for him. A man of maturer years leaped out of his chair and began to stutter. He did not utter a distinct syllable, but as fast as tongue would work, he said, 'tut-tut-tut-tut-tut.' This was evidence he had his 'baptism'. The woman who had on the silk waist appeared again, this time singing a far away tune that sounded very unnatural and repulsive...When the altar call was made, a woman walked up to the front and kissed a man...kissing between the sexes is a common occurrence in the tongues meetings."* ('Demons and Tongues', pp. 71-73, A. White).

Another witness to these meetings, where disorder and confusion reigned, had this to report: *"Our missionaries have been stationed at Los Angeles* (where the Azusa St. meetings were held),*during the whole history of the Tongues movement, and have watched it closely from the very first outbreak in Seymour's meetings; and truly, conditions have been such that it would be impossible to publish the things that have occurred there. The familiarity between sexes in the public meetings has been shocking, to say the least. Hell has reaped an awful harvest and infidelity has become more strongly rooted on the Pacific coast than ever before."* ('Demons and Tongues', p. 82).

The 'Dictionary of Pentecostal and Charismatic Movements', reporting on William J. Seymour, co-founder of Pentecostalism and pastor of the Azusa St. Mission, said, *"Seymour* *moved away from a theology of tongues as the initial physical evidence of baptism in the Spirit. <u>In point of fact, Seymour ultimately repudiated the "initial evidence" teaching</u>* (speaking in <u>tongues</u>) *as providing "an open door for witches and spiritualists and free-lovism".* " (p.36). Strange, those who spoke in tongues in the Bible did not have any trouble with witches or the like at their meetings. *"Azusa was typically described by the press as a 'colored' congregation that met in a 'tumble-down shack' and made the night 'hideous' through the 'howlings of the worshippers'..."* (p.36). Seymour's co-founder, Charles Parham, concluded the following: *"Never were God's servants surrounded with more deceptive counterfeits of real divine experience than in this day and age...the magician's work is so well nigh perfect, that it often is indeed hard to distinguish the true and the false...I have witnessed great dangers in the work here in Los Angeles, and in pointing them out I shall not refer to individuals, but to the work itself as a whole, so that we all may see the error of our way and get back to God."* ('The Life Of Charles Parham', pp. 166-167). And this from the *leaders* of events that are held in as high regard today as those which occurred on the day of Pentecost, by those who have perpetuated such ungodly events. Now it is one thing to shrug off the critiques of those exposing Pentecostal or Charismatic movements, but to ignore, or choose to remain ignorant of, the very warnings of the leaders who co-founded

Pentecostalism and to choose to continue the traditions and practices, which these leaders themselves condemned, is utter stupidity.

One of, if not the most, disturbing aspect of these meetings at Azusa St., which many today ignorantly and blasphemously hold to as equal to the events of the day of Pentecost as recorded in the Scriptures, may be seen in the following accounts: "_...spiritualists and mediums from the numerous occult societies of Los Angeles began to attend and contribute their seances and trances to the service.._ _Disturbed by these developments, Seymour wrote to Parham (his spiritual father) for advice on how to handle 'the spirits' and begged him to come to Los Angeles and take over supervision of the revival._" ('The Holiness Pentecostal Movement in the United States', p.110). "_W.J. Seymour was still writing urgent letters appealing for help, as spiritualistic manifestations, hypnotic forces and fleshly contortions as known in the colored Camp meetings in the South, had broken loose in the meetings._" ('The Life Of Charles Parham', p.156). Does any of this sound even remotely like a description of meetings between true Christians in the Bible? Of course not! Unlike the Azusa St. meetings, which not only attracted spiritualists and mediums and the like, but saw them actually take an active and not insignificant part in the meetings, we see that the outpouring of God's one and only Holy Spirit on the day of Pentecost resulted in the following, as is recorded for us in Acts 5:12,13: **"And by the hands of the** *apostles were many signs and wonders wrought among the people; (and they were all with one accord in Solomon's Porch. <u>And of the rest durst no man join himself to them:</u> but the people magnified them."* No medium or witch dared to approach the Holy Spirit who was resident in the apostles who were performing genuine miracles by the power of the Holy Spirit. **Rather than be a place to avoid, the meetings at Azusa Street were, in reality, a Mecca for spiritualists, witches and mediums alike!** Merely because these facts are little known and rarely reported does not alter the fact that they are all documented and verifiable, historical **FACT!!**

The final comments from the pen of Azusa Street founder, Charles F. Parham, should resound in the minds of every charismatic today as they begin to see, and come to terms with, the corrupt foundation upon which their movement is based: *"Let me speak plainly with regard to the work as I have found it here. I found hypnotic influences, familiar spirit influences, spiritualistic influences, mesmeric influences and all kinds of spells and spasms, falling in trances etc. All of these things are foreign to and unknown in the movement (the Apostolic Faith movement) outside of Los Angeles, except in the places visited by the workers sent out from this city."* ('The Life Of Charles Parham', p. 168). Parham added: *"After preaching two or three times, I was informed by two of the elders, one who was a hypnotist (I had seen him lay his hands on many who came through chattering, jabbering, speaking no language at all) that I was not wanted in this place"* ('The Life Of Charles Parham', p. 163). I doubt whether there are very many Charismatics at all who are aware of the controversy and very un-Christian occurrences which characterized the infamous Azusa St. meetings.

The Dictionary of Pentecostal and Charismatic Movements informs us that: *"There is now historical evidence to suggest that the Azusa St. revival was no more than confirmation of a phenomenon that had already begun among Black Holiness-Pentecostals"*(p.80).

"Many former charismatics, including pastors, have renounced what they had at first believed were true gifts of the Holy Spirit. It is seldom realized that there are many former charismatics and pentecostals who have reassessed the whole issue in terms of Scripture, experience and history and have turned their back on the claims of a modern-day revival of biblical gifts. A former Pentecostal pastor of 25 years, G.E. Gardner, declared, *"I have heard hundreds of messages in tongues, and interpretations. Not one has ever added anything of value to the meeting"* ('The Corinthian Catastrophe', p.53). Gardner adds that the seeking of these modern charismatic experiences is *'never harmless'* ('The Corinthian Catastrophe', p.55).

One of the most moving testimonies in this regard comes from a man who spent over 20 years in the pentecostal atmosphere of the Apostolic Faith Mission, Full Gospel Church and

Assemblies of God, attending and assisting major campaigns by various leaders. He wrote: *"I laid hands on the sick. I rebuked death. I prophesied. I spoke in tongues. I interpreted. I would say now, in all sincerity, that I saw and experienced nothing which would lead me to believe that Pentecostalism offers ANYTHING along the lines of the New Testament Church's experience"* ('Reformation Today', Oct/Nov. 1973, K. Haarnhof, p.20). The above quoted Pentecostal minister acknowledges that there are many sincere people in the Charismatic and Pentecostal movements, but his conclusions and his exposure of the *'faulty doctrinal basis, manipulative indoctrination'* and *'charged atmosphere'* remain firm. **Sincerity can never be the evidence that substantiates what one is zealous for as being of God. And a zeal without right knowledge can never be of, or lead to, the true God (see Rom. 10:1-4). No one is saved because of zeal alone, or by sincerity alone, but only if one has been given the gift of the love of the truth that is revealed by God in His mighty Gospel.**

As can be clearly and immediately observed by the discerning believer in whom God's Word and Spirit reside, these meetings at Azusa St., which initiated the first wave of modern-day charismania upon the world, were far from God-ordained. The meetings were clearly a satanic counterfeit of the wonderful events that occurred on the one and only birthday of the Christian Church: the day of Pentecost as described in the book of Acts. The Azusa St. meetings were not only a hive of satanic experiences and a spiritual free-for-all, but importantly, these experiences, which millions of people are seeking even today, also gave credibility to false gospels and the acceptance of such in the minds and hearts of their recipients. **God's Gospel was never preached at Azusa Street and the Holy Spirit, therefore, never performed any work there.** Nevertheless, the facts and the Scriptures were thrown to the wind as, from this unsightly and unscriptural mess, the Pentecostal movement grew and grew and later became popularly referred to, in the mid-1960's, as the Charismatic movement.

One New Testament scholar has made the following observation: *"Too long Christians have assumed that the non-charismatic must produce incontestable biblical evidence that the miraculous sign gifts did cease. However, non-charismatics have no burden to prove this, since it has already been proved by history. It is an irrefutable fact admitted by many Pentecostals. Therefore the charismatics must prove biblically that the sign gifts will start up again during the Church Age and that today's phenomena are this reoccurrence. In other words, they must prove that their experiences are the reoccurrence of gifts that have not occurred for almost 1900 years."* ('The Cessation Of The Sign Gifts', p. 374). While this is a very good point, it would be a rather futile exercise seeing that the Gospel has never once been preached by these charismatic groups, who place so much emphasis on their signs and wonders rather than on the Person and Work of Jesus Christ. **The signs and wonders are really only the tip of the iceberg. What the even greater evil in all this Pentecostal and Charismatic chaos is, is the fact that amid all the excitement and smiling faces and the ecstatic experiences, the Gospel is not being preached and therefore no one is being saved.** People have simply been hoodwinked, by all the activity and ecstatic hullabaloo occurring within Pentecostalism and Charismaticism, into believing that because all is being done in the name of Jesus, these movements are sanctioned by God Himself and all involved are Christians. **Nothing could be further from the truth!** If there is no Gospel, that is, God's Gospel, then it is not a Christian gathering and any phenomena present is anything but Christian. The Scriptures state clearly in 2 John 9 that ***"Whosoever transgresseth and abideth not in the doctrine of Christ, HATH NOT GOD..."*** If *individuals* who hold not to God's Gospel have not God, what makes anyone think that a gathering of such people is attended, ordered and supported, by God? The math is quite simple: **NO GOSPEL - NO GOD!!**

In light of all the evidence presented, we can only conclude that though there are many sincere people in the Charismatic movement, the movement itself cannot be of God, for all the 'gifts', all the 'signs', all the 'wonders' it lays claim to are just as flawed and riddled with imperfection as those that are common to every like cult that has preceded it. This movement is nothing new, just the latest and largest of its kind. **There is no true Gospel accompanying any of these lying signs and wonders, so how can God be the one behind them?** What would be the point of all these signs and wonders if the people experiencing them are not being taught the truth and being saved? I suggest that, rather than tearing this book up in anger and frustration at this point, the charismatic have courage enough to read this author's book 'The Blasphemy Against the Holy Spirit', of which this book is but a chapter, and learn some more startling facts about the movement he so zealously seeks to defend, and be a part of.

IS IT THE SAME SPIRIT?

The Roman Catholic Charismatic Renewal continues to grow at a rapid pace. All around the world, Roman Catholics are experiencing the Charismatic's second baptism known as the 'baptism of the Holy Spirit'. Statistics show that at least half the Charismatics in the world are also Roman Catholic. Many Roman Catholics are being 'slain in the spirit' and are 'speaking in tongues'. Much of the Roman Catholic priesthood has embraced the 'charismatic experience' which, incidentally, has received the Pope's official blessing. But what does all this mean? How can Roman Catholics be experiencing what has generally been thought to be experiences found exclusively within what is considered to be a Protestant movement? The question we will be addressing is: *'Is the spirit that is granting Charismatics their experiences – 'tongues', the 'slaying' etc – the same spirit that Roman Catholics joyfully receive?'*

Before we examine the question *'Is it the same spirit?'*, it is important that we look at what most people have presumed to be Protestant, namely the Pentecostal and Charismatic movements. This despite the fact that both abide in the doctrines of Arminianism which stem from Pelagianism, a fifth-century heresy that continues today, in which the Roman Catholic concept of salvation is rooted.

1971 was the year that saw the emergence of what became a very influential book. Entitled 'The Pentecostal Movement in the (Roman) Catholic Church', it was authored by a Roman Catholic priest named Edward D. O'Connor. The book became recognized as a classic and is still considered so by the Vatican and Roman Catholic activists. On page 23 of the book, O'Connor makes the following statement: *"Although they derive from Protestant backgrounds, the Pentecostal churches are not typically Protestant in their belief, attitudes or practices. Many historians, as well as many of their own members, regard them as a 'third force' in the Christian world, between Protestantism and* (Roman) *Catholicism."*

We also see in further quotes from this book the compatibility of Roman Catholicism and Charismaticism. *"*(Roman) *Catholics who have accepted Pentecostal spirituality have found it to be fully in harmony with their traditional faith and life. They experience it not as a borrowing from an alien religion, but as a connatural—meaning to have a similar nature or origin—development of their own"* (p.28).

"The spiritual experience of those who have been touched by the grace of the Holy Spirit in the Pentecostal movement is in profound harmony with the classical spirit of theology of the (Roman Catholic) *Church"* (p.183). And, *"...the doctrine that is developing in the Pentecostal churches today, seems to be going through stages very similar to those which occurred in the early Middle*

Ages when the classical doctrine was taking shape" (p.193,194).

We learn from this the fact that the Roman Catholic Church sees no threat from the Charismatic movement, but has officially approved and embraced it, and is receptive to its 'blessings'. However, Roman Catholic doctrine is NOT changing! Roman Catholics more than ever are remaining faithful to the use of the Rosary, prayers to Mary and other false Roman doctrines and practices.

For years many have believed that true revival has been occurring, firstly through the Pentecostal movement and later the Charismatic movement and that these two movements have seen the great move of God in these last days. And yet we see these 'great movements' now walking hand in hand with Romanism and other proponents of erroneous doctrine! They have become great friends. Some would even call it a family reunion. Roman Catholicism and the Charismatic Movement, specifically the Assemblies Of God churches, have played a major part in formulating the one-world church via the Ecumenical Movement.

Wilson Ewin, author of the book 'The Pied Piper of the Pentecostal Movement', says, *"Untold millions of Catholic Pentecostals are now among the faithful of the Vatican. They are distinguished not only by the Pentecostal experience but also by their unswerving loyalty to the dogmas and teachings of the Roman Church. Medieval Catholicism as defined by the Council of Trent, remains intact in their hearts"* (p.25). Ewin adds, *"The very powers of classical Pentecostalism are now being shared with Roman Catholic Pentecostalists. And this of course, without conversion to Christ. The exploits of Oral Roberts, Kathryn Kuhlman, Rex Humbard, Aimee Semple McPherson, David Du Plessis and other mainline Pentecostal stars are even being outpaced by some Roman Catholic Pentecostalists"* (p.26).

Throughout his book, Ewin tells of large meetings being held by Roman Catholics and Pentecostals. *"Meetings have been carried on for many years between Vatican authorities and Pentecostal leaders. Cardinal Leon Suenens, usually involved in this, spoke at the 1977 Congress in Kansas City. He and 'Thomas Zimmerman (Assemblies of God), J.O. Patterson (Church of God in Christ), and Archbishop Bill Burnett (Anglican) stood together before the vast multitude in an unprecedented demonstration of unity'"* (p.34).

There still exists somewhat of a doctrinal gulf between Roman Catholics and Charismatics but these have been put to one side as they enjoy an experience-based unity. The Assemblies of God churches and the Vatican both agree that it is God's Holy Spirit who is at work in both the Charismatic Movement and Roman Catholicism. And yet, when we examine the testimonies of Roman Catholics who have experienced charismatic phenomena such as 'tongues', the 'slaying' and the 'baptism of the Holy Spirit'—a term not found in the Scriptures— we see that they are not, in turn, being led out of the errors of Romanism but deeper into them! One such testimony specifically records that the person began to pray the Rosary, *"a practice"* they said, *"I have taken up since the baptism in the spirit"* (Catholic Pentecostals, p.68). Another wrote of his renewed allegiance to Mary. A priest declared after his 'baptism in the spirit', *"Never before had I such a sense of Mary's role in leading me into the fullness of Christ and the Spirit"* (The Charismatic Renewal and the Irish Experience, p.92). In fact, some nominal Roman Catholics who were not amongst those who prayed to Mary or prayed the Rosary or even attended Mass, now eagerly do so as a direct result of their charismatic experience!

E.N. Gross in his book 'Miracles, Demons and Spiritual Warfare' says, *"The Charismatic Movement now embraces Roman Catholics with a total openness. Basic differences of doctrine no longer seem to matter. Huge Charismatic meetings feature Protestant and Roman Catholic speakers as if there were no difference between them. 'Tongues', 'prophecies', 'healings' abound in such meetings—all with loud united shouts of 'amen' and 'praise Jesus'"* (p.160).

If it is the Holy Spirit giving these experiences to Roman Catholics, how then are we to explain the fact that these people are not being led out of Romanism and renouncing her blasphemous teachings but are becoming more firmly entrenched in her heretical doctrines? The Bible says that the Holy Spirit is the Spirit of Truth and the Lord Jesus Christ further stated that ***"...when He, the Spirit of Truth, is come, He will guide you into all truth..."*** (Jn. 16:13). He would not confirm and establish Roman Catholics or any other followers of false doctrine in their error but would lead them out of it. And the Holy Spirit would certainly not lead God's people to join hands with those who are steeped in deadly error, having embraced a false gospel. But wait, we need to ask these questions at this point: *'How can the spirit that is active in both the Pentecostal and Charismatic movements be the Holy Spirit of God when this spirit has not led the followers of either of these movements to the Gospel of Christ but to a counterfeit and has fused these movements with the giant of doctrinal monsters, the Roman Catholic Church? How can it be the Holy Spirit leading these people when their unity is not over the doctrine of Christ but rather involves a disregard of doctrine?'* These movements have entered into an experience-based love affair with Roman Catholicism and even Mormonism through the Promise Keepers movement.

Jesus Christ said that the Holy Spirit, Whom He called ***"the Spirit of truth"*** three times in the Gospel of John, would guide all God's chosen into all truth (Jn. 16:13). The spirit which is at work in the Charismatic Movement and Roman Catholicism **IS** the same spirit but is **NOT** the Holy Spirit, for this counterfeit spirit is not leading people into all truth. He is not leading them to the only Gospel of God which reveals the Righteousness of Christ and which declares that

Christ's death was for all those God gave Him, but is encouraging fellowship with error and leading people into a false unity—love and experiences—rather than Biblical unity (which God Almighty is the Author of) which is, and can only ever be, love **and** truth. Disciples of both groups need to be aware of the Scriptural truth that doctrine must never be laid aside, even because of an overwhelming desire to unite at any cost. **Only those who believe the True Gospel can be of the same mind as the Scriptures when it comes to Who Christ is, what Christ has done and for whom He has done it.**

The sight of the Charismatic Movement and the Roman Catholic Church merging ever closer by the minute and, although in disagreement over some doctrine, warmly welcoming the spirit which is leading them deeper into ecumenical bondage and doctrine which is at odds with the Scriptures, demonstrates conclusively that it **IS** one and the same spirit—but it is **NOT** the Holy Spirit of God, it is a foul counterfeit. A counterfeit which is titillating the senses and feeding an insatiable urge to see and feel and experience something out of the ordinary — to have a man-made unity now, based on experience and not Truth, rather than the true unity which only Jesus Christ brings to all those who abide in HIS doctrine (see 2 Jn. 9). God's Holy Word states that the Christian's walk is one of faith, not of sight (2 Cor. 5:7). God has chosen to speak to His people through the written Word and it is in the Holy Scriptures that you will find true experience with God, not in some flesh-pleasing titillation dripping with false doctrine.

In John's First Letter, chapter 4 and verse 1, we see his instruction to **"...believe not every spirit, but try the spirits whether they are of God: because many false prophets are gone out into the world."** Many today do not question, but merely accept at face value that if an experience is real and seemingly 'beneficial', it *must* be of God thus giving credibility to, in the minds of such thinkers, whatever movement one has had the experience in. It is clear that the spirit working within the Charismatic movement is leading it further into fellowship with darkness. This same spirit is not guiding Roman Catholics into all truth but deeper into the heresies of Romanism. **Therefore this spirit cannot be the Holy Spirit of God but is the unholy spirit of Satan.** God's people—those among His elect currently a part of the Roman Catholic Church or the Pentecostal or Charismatic movements who do not yet believe the Gospel must do so—need to come out of the Roman Catholic Church and the Charismatic and Pentecostal movements according to Revelation 18:4, **"...that ye be not partakers of her sins, and that ye receive not of her plagues."** The line has been most distinctly marked out: will you follow the spirit of the Charismatic movement and the Roman Catholic Church or will you follow the Holy Spirit of God who guides people into all Truth?

The Spirit of God is the Spirit of Truth and He alone it is Who will guide people into His truth:

the Gospel of Jesus Christ. **We exhort Roman Catholics and Charismatics alike to study the Word of God and experience the TRUTH!**

THE FATAL ERROR OF BELIEVING A FALSE GOSPEL

The reason it is a fatal error not to believe the truth of Gospel essentials such as sovereign election by the free grace and will of God, the substitutionary atonement of Jesus Christ, the eternal security of the man whom God has elected unto salvation and for whom Christ has died, and that unless one is submitted to the Righteousness of Christ one cannot be saved, is that **not believing these truths, or even being undecided, shows that one is believing something other than the Truth of God which, naturally, would contradict His truth. That which does not come from God is that which opposes Him and what He has said. The person who believes in that which God has not said is in ignorance/darkness, which is what a person in a saved state is brought**

out from in the first place. Either way, they are not believing the Truth.

Belief of the truth, which is revealed in the doctrine of God and in which every true believer abides (2 Jn. 9), is what distinguishes a saved person, who has been brought out of darkness into God's marvellous Light, from a person who is lost and sitting in darkness. The state of every man by nature is shown clearly in the following verse: ***"Having the understanding darkened, being alienated from the life of God through the ignorance that is in them, because of the blindness of their heart"*** (Eph. 4:18 cf. Jn. 1:5). **The blinded heart cannot pump the blood of eternal life. None are born again who remain in darkness and ignorance of what the Gospel is: *"...if our Gospel be hid, it is hid to them that are lost"*** (2 Cor. 4:3). If the Gospel is hid to any man, he cannot see it and he is therefore ignorant of it. This is evidence that he is lost, for God has not revealed His truth to Him. The truth of God is revealed to His elect, and to others it is not given: ***"...it is given unto you to know the mysteries of the kingdom of heaven, but to them it is not given....he that received seed into the good ground is he that heareth the word, and understandeth it"*** (Matt. 13:11,23). Just as in physical birth one is brought out of darkness (the womb), so too, in spiritual birth one is brought out of darkness (ignorance of the truth) into God's marvellous Light—His Truth.**Ignorance is an unmistakeable sign of lostness.** Ignorance is the womb, if you will, from which a man receives no sustenance but is brought out of when he is given birth to by God through His Truth (Jas. 1:18).

The Bible teaches that one cannot believe in the true Christ whilst in ignorance of Who He is and what He has done.**One is not born as long as one is in the womb—one is not born again as long as one is in ignorance.** Only*after* one has heard of the true Christ can one rightly claim to believe in Him: ***"In Whom*** (Christ) ***ye also trusted, AFTER that ye heard the Word of Truth, THE GOSPEL of your salvation: in Whom also AFTER that ye believed, ye were sealed with that Holy Spirit of promise"*** (Eph. 1:13). This Scripture shows beyond a shadow of a doubt that one cannot believe in the true Christ **who has not had that Christ revealed to them** via the word of truth, His doctrine: His Gospel. The only hope for sinners is revealed in God's Gospel Message: ***"For the hope which is laid up for you in heaven, whereof ye heard before IN THE WORD OF THE TRUTH OF THE***

GOSPEL" (Col. 1:5). The message of the sure hope of Heaven lies in the doctrines of the Gospel and none can bear fruit unto God before **they hear His Gospel and know** the grace of God **IN TRUTH** (see Col. 1:6 cf. Matt. 13:23). One cannot believe and trust in Christ until *after* one has *heard* His Gospel and none are sealed with that Holy Spirit of promise who have not *believed* that glorious Gospel, wherein Christ and His Righteousness are revealed, and rejected **all** others (Rom. 1:16,17).

One cannot have true saving God-given Faith if one does not believe the one, true, God-given Gospel. One cannot have true saving faith if one believes that one was saved whilst believing in another gospel, because true saving faith trusts only in one Gospel and believes only one Gospel to be the truth, and only one Gospel that can save. This would be like a person who wrongly imagined twelve inches to be a certain length, then upon discovering how long twelve inches really was, **nevertheless insisting that their previous appraisal was just as accurate as that deemed by the ruler!** None are saved whilst insisting they were saved *before* hearing and 'believing' THE Gospel, for the very Gospel of God which such people claim to believe denies that such a thing is possible! Such people often base their salvation on a variety of experiences and see such life-changing and morally reforming episodes as unquestionable proof of spiritual rebirth, despite the absence of the Seed of God by which a man is born again: the Gospel! **God recognises only one Gospel as His and so do all His people.** The Gospel of God will have no part of a person who professes his love for it and yet is *married* to another gospel. Imagine getting married to a person who insists on bringing along their previous husband/wife!! **One must be dead to all other gospels before one can savingly and rightly be joined to God's Gospel. The Gospel of God cannot be yoked together with someone who believes they were saved prior to hearing and believing it and who will not reject every other gospel they previously believed in.** This would be like having two wives—a case of spiritual bigamy if you will. Equally, none are saved who insist that such a person is saved or who says a person that has not heard or does not believe THE Gospel is saved regardless. **For they are saying—contrary to what the Gospel declares—that one can be ignorant of the Gospel—wilfully or otherwise—and be nonetheless saved. Salvation, then, would be something based on a person's sincerity and 'genuine desire**

for God' rather than on God's genuine love for a person, shown by His revealing His Gospel to them and providing them with the faith to believe it. Any gospel that is not THE Gospel simply cannot save. *"He that believeth and is baptized shall be saved; but he that believeth not shall be damned"* (Mk. 16:16).

There is no contingency plan of salvation for those who believe error about Christ. There is no likelihood that any of God's chosen will not believe His Gospel in its entirety. One hireling informed this author that he does not know how much error God is willing to put up with in His people. The answer is: **no error that contributes to the perversion of the Gospel of Christ, thereby revealing another gospel that God has not declared and another christ that God does not claim to be HIS Son**, will be tolerated. Error is the spoiler. Error is the leaven that leaveneth the whole lump. **God never overlooks the error that leavens the whole lump** (see Gal 5:9). **Fatal error is that which changes truth into a lie and THE Gospel into <u>another</u> gospel.** No one has ever been saved by acknowledging error! **Heaven is for lovers of the truth, not those who are enamoured with a lie.** Those who believe a lie, ie. another gospel, far from being saved, are under strong delusion (2 Thess. 2:11). There are no allowances made in God's plan of salvation for those who believe error, for the whole idea of that Great Plan is that it be believed in order that people be saved. **Knowledge of God's Truth is the fulfilment of God's Plan for the salvation of His people.**

Saving faith ALWAYS believes THE TRUE Gospel, never a false one, for it is the faith that comes from God (2 Thess. 2:13,14). The faith which does not save, which does not come from God as His gift, is that which believes salvation can either come before or without belief in God's only Gospel. **The Faith that God gives finds refuge, comfort and security ONLY in the doctrine of Christ. The faith that finds refuge, comfort and security in anything other than the doctrine of Christ ALONE hasn't come from God.**

The majority of this article was excerpted from the author's book 'Election Is Just Not Fair!'

Please Contact:

morenodalbello@yahoo.com.au

Please Visit:

www.godsonlygospel.com

Made in the USA
Monee, IL
08 July 2026